Lea

MW01596446

Ten Life Lessons I Wish
I Had Learned Sooner

Mark R. Lile

DEDICATION

This book is dedicated to my wife and best friend Janet, who has always been my biggest fan and supporter, and has always believed in me.

CONTENTS

INTRODUCTION

Hidden within the psyche of every individual is a desire to live a life of meaning and purpose that will leave a great legacy. Nobody wants to be insignificant. Everyone wants to feel as if their life has been of value. Many live their entire life never discovering the gifts that lie dormant inside them. Without a sense of purpose, life will drive a person to despair. I am a firm believer that God has a plan and a purpose for everyone's life.

When God created man, He knew man could not thrive living alone. After God created the Heavens and the Earth, He surveyed everything that was created and concluded that it *was good*. However, after creating man, God saw in His divine wisdom it *was not* good for man to be alone. The Bible tells us in Genesis 2:18, "The Lord God said, 'It is not good for man to be alone. I will make a helper suitable for him.' " (New International Version) God created mankind to be social, love one another, and invest into the lives of other people. We were created with the potential of making a positive impact in the lives of others.

I chose the title of this book to be *Leaving a Legacy* because everyone will leave a legacy behind when they die. A legacy is a story and set of values which characterizes a person's life. Your legacy will continue to be played out in the lives of your friends and family after you are gone. When you die it is not what you leave *to* your friends and family that counts, but what you leave *in* them. Think about the storyline of your life. What legacy are you leaving to your friends and family?

At the risk of being morbid, imagine yourself being able to hear the conversations of people at your funeral. What would they say about your life? Many people leave behind a legacy of addiction, abuse, dishonesty, and immorality. They leave behind countless reminders of emotional scars and pain they have inflicted upon others during their lifetime. On the positive side, others go through life being game-changers and difference-makers. These are the selfless ones. They are encouragers, motivators, and have a passion for helping others. Take an honest look at your life at this point and ask yourself which person you are. If you were to die today, what legacy would you leave to those around you?

The legacy we create is tied to decisions and choices we make throughout life. Everyone has reflected over past periods of their life. Often many say, "I wish I had…" or "I wish I hadn't…" Have you ever wished you could rewind the tape of your life and play it back differently? We wish we could use wisdom we've gained to erase our mistakes. Mistakes we make throughout our life serve a purpose. Our mistakes teach us valuable lessons of life. Life's lessons will make us better people and direct us to our God-given destiny if we will learn from them.

Life is too short to focus on past mistakes. It is important to not focus our thoughts on past mistakes, but also never forget the lessons we learned. In the Bible in Philippians 3:13, the Apostle Paul said, "Brothers and sisters, I do not consider myself to have taken hold of it.; but one thing I do; forgetting what is behind and straining toward what is ahead. I press on toward the goal to win the prize for which God has called me Heavenward in Christ Jesus." (New International Version) Paul chose not to focus on the mistakes he had made. Instead, he used the lessons from his past mistakes to help him fulfill the purpose God had for him.

Looking back at your past mistakes, you may think it too late for you to leave a great legacy. Everyone makes mistakes, but until you breathe your last breath, the book of your life you are writing is not finished. Regardless of how disappointing or painful the first chapters of your life have been, you still hold the pen. You still have the power to write how your story will end and the legacy you will leave to your friends and family.

One of my favorite movies is *The Shawshank Redemption*. If you have seen the movie, you know that it is about a man named Andy Dufresne, played by Timothy Robbins. Andy spends a long time in prison for a crime he didn't commit. During the years of his prison stay, he befriends a man the inmates call "Red", played by Morgan Freeman. In one particular scene in the movie, Andy dreams about a life in Mexico and asks Red, "Do you know what the Mexicans say about the Pacific? They say it has no memory. That's where I want to live the rest of my life; a place that's warm with no memories." Red looks on and says, "I don't think I could make it on the outside Andy. I've been in here most of my life. I'm an institutional man now." Andy ends with, "It comes down to a simple choice; get busy living or get busy dying." That is a profound statement that applies to us all! Many people in life become so institutionalized by their situation, regret over past mistakes, or their circumstances, it causes them to stop chasing their dream. Life without hope is a prison. If we allow ourselves to, and are not careful, we can spend so much time focusing on our past failures and mistakes it paralyzes us. It is then we accept living in the prison of regret and we get busy dying.

In this book, I will share lessons of life I learned because of making many mistakes. Included will be passages of Bible scripture applicable to the topic. As a Christian, I believe it is impossible to reach your full potential apart from a life led by God. If you don't believe the Bible has answers to life's problems, this book isn't for you. Many of the lessons I have learned resulted from God speaking to me through his written word.

As you read this book you may realize you are making the same mistakes I have made. Most wisdom won't come from times of success. Wisdom comes from times you make mistakes and learn from them. My prayer is as you read this book it will speak to you in your particular situation in life. It is through God and life's lessons you can change your destiny. It's not too late to start afresh! Life's most valuable lessons will help you leave a legacy which will have a positive impact on your friends and family for generations to come.

LESSON # 1
DON'T STRESS OUT TRYING TO FIT IN

As a child growing up in Wood River, Illinois, I struggled to fit in with my peers. Looking back, I remember how isolated I felt. I was never one of the popular kids in school. You can recall how things were back in the days of junior high and high school. Four identifiable social groups were present. There were the jocks, the honor roll brainy kids, the preppy student council kids, and the always in trouble drug using kids. As the saying goes, birds of a feather flock together. As kids in school, we only interacted with kids in our own social groups.

Like many others, I didn't fit into any of the four social groups during my years in school. Since I missed out on being able to play sports for a good piece of my youth, I wasn't a jock. My grades were never great, so I didn't fit in with the "brainy" kids. Being shy and insecure, I didn't fit in with the preppy student council crowd. My parents were two very devout Christians, so I was far from being the always in trouble drug using kid. However, I went through a short spell during my freshman year experimenting with marijuana. It was nothing more than a desperate attempt to fit in somewhere.

From age 8 to age 13, I wore a Milwaukee brace to treat scoliosis. It was a horrible looking and uncomfortable contraption I had to wear 23 hours a day. If you do an internet image search of the words "Milwaukee Brace", you will get a vivid picture. You will see the mess of leather, steel, and plastic that encased me from my hips to my neck. I still remember the day I got that brace. I was a patient at Shriners Hospital in St. Louis, Missouri and it was my eighth birthday. A brace wasn't on my birthday wish list. Looking back, I realize those years played a part in turning me into the shy, insecure, kid I used to be. I remember the stares and ridicule I endured from other kids during those years

During my days growing up, I was insecure because I felt I was always being stared at by others. Other kids were curious about the metal under my shirt. I didn't fit in anywhere. Staying concerned what others thought of me kept my self-esteem depleted. There were days I wished I could have worn a sign explaining the reason for the brace. I grew very weary of answering questions.

By the time my treatment for scoliosis ended in the summer of 1977, my self-esteem was in shambles. It was during the early summer between eighth grade and my freshman year in high school that the body cast I was wearing was removed. The cast started at my hips and went to right under my chin. The cast (which was changed three times over nine months), was required after I had a spinal fusion of my thoracic vertebrae nine months earlier. I will never forget the necktie and shirt buttons that my youngest sister Dee helped me draw on the chest area of my cast using colorful markers. I suppose it was my best attempt at being light-hearted and jovial about wearing a cast that was very uncomfortable.

During that summer, I remember how happy I was to be out of the cast. I remember the relief of knowing my scoliosis treatment was over after six years. Part of what I wanted had materialized. At last I looked like any other typical thirteen year old kid. I *looked* like everybody else, but because my self-esteem had deteriorated over the previous six years, I did not *feel* like everyone else. I continued to embrace the mindset I was something inferior to all of my peers.

As I matured, I realized one of the biggest mistakes we make in life is trying to be like everyone else. I remember a quote that says, "Why fit in when you were born to stand out?" One of the best things you can do is love yourself and not feel the need to pattern yourself to fit the mold of someone else's expectations.

The society in which we live today tries to force upon us a distorted picture of what makes up success. Masses of people today see relationships and marriages portrayed on television and in the theaters. When they do, they are often lured into believing what they are seeing is the mold they must fit into if they are to succeed in a relationship. Glamour and fashion magazines have pictures of models that are digitally enhanced to make them appear to have flawless features. Countless numbers of young women today are being led to believe being physically fit is looking like the model on the cover of *Vogue* or *Glamour*. When these young women fail to match their appearances to the photos of models they see, many become depressed. Many feel like they are less than beautiful and often develop eating disorders like anorexia or bulimia. This happens because they are being deceived by a distorted picture of beauty.

We live in a materialistic world driven by a thirst for money, possessions, and power. Society today doesn't use the values of honesty, integrity, and a happy family as the meter to gauge success. In today's world, success is often based on the size of a person's financial portfolio more than by a person's efforts to help their fellow man. Society tries to tell us we are a success when we have a massive house, drive the finest cars, and have a six-figure income. Often when people fail to fit into the materialistic and unrealistic mold of success being thrown at them, they feel like a failure, and believe they don't measure up to the standards being set by society.

There are groups where you won't fit. As hard as you may try to mingle and socialize with certain groups of people, you come to realize that you don't fit into that environment. It is like trying to place a square peg into a round hole. Not fitting in doesn't mean you are inferior. It means your values and priorities are different; and that's ok. As individuals we get ourselves into trouble when we try to force ourselves into a mold where we don't belong and try being something we are not. The late actress Judy Garland once said, "Always be a first-rate version of yourself, not a second-rate version of someone else." We don't have to fit in.

There is a great story from the Bible of a man who based on the opinions of his Father and his brothers didn't fit the mold. He was the baby of the family; the youngest of eight brothers. His name was David. In the story in the sixteenth chapter of 1 Samuel, God instructed the prophet Samuel to travel to the village of Bethlehem. He was to pay a visit to a man named Jesse. God told Samuel that he would anoint one of Jesse's sons to be king.

When Samuel arrived in Bethlehem and appeared before Jesse, he asked Jesse to bring all of his sons before him. The first of Jesse's sons that Samuel saw was Eliab. When Eliab stepped before Samuel, Samuel reasoned to himself, "This must be the one that God wants me to anoint as king." Eliab was a tall, rugged looking, seasoned man of war. But, God spoke to Samuel and said, "Nope, he may look how you think a king should look, but he's not the one."

The next son of Jesse to pass before Samuel was Abinadab. (Don't you love these names? Imagine naming your son or maybe your dog Abinadab. That could be a fun conversation starter.) When Abinadab passed before Samuel, God again let Samuel know that he was not the one who should be anointed king.

The little pageant of Jesse's sons continued until seven of the sons of Jesse had strutted their stuff in front of Samuel. After the seven had passed in front of Samuel, he said to Jesse, "None of these guys are who God wants to be king. Don't you have anymore more sons?" Reluctantly, Jesse told

Samuel, "Well, there is my youngest son, but he's busy tending sheep." Yes, the baby of the family and runt kid of the bunch was a shepherd. He was not skilled in the tactics of combat and warfare; he was a shepherd. Jesse thought to himself, "Surely there's no possible way you would consider anointing him king." Samuel spoke up and said to Jesse, "Go get him! We will not sit until he gets here!" Within a short time, David appeared on the scene. The kid that was watching sheep on the hillsides and pastures of Bethlehem was then standing before Samuel. As soon as Samuel saw David, God spoke to Samuel and said, "Yep, he's the one! Anoint him as king!"

Think about this story for a moment. Compared to all of David's brothers, he seemed like an outcast. He did not fit. He did not look like his brothers. He didn't act like his brothers. From an appearance standpoint, he didn't fit the expected mold of what a king should be. Of the sons of Jesse, David was the one who didn't fit in. It reminds me of that old song we used to hear on *Sesame Street*. The song said, "One of these things is not like the others. One of these things just doesn't belong." David appeared as if he didn't belong with the others.

Unlike me when I was a kid, David didn't get stressed out

because he didn't fit in. As a kid, I wanted validation from others. I wanted someone to give me their seal of approval. David *knew* who he was. He had spent many a day in the presence of God while tending to his flocks on the hills of Bethlehem. David wasn't looking to his father, his brothers, or anyone else to gain a sense of self-worth. He looked to God to discover his life's purpose.

The Bible tells us David was a man after God's own heart. David had a passion for seeking God's approval. You get yourself into trouble when you spend time seeking validation and approval from others. Seek to find out what God says about you. God loves you. You are his masterpiece!

David knew how God felt about him. I love what David said to God in Psalm 139:13-14 of the Bible. David was speaking to God when he said, "You created my inmost being; you knit me together in my mother's womb. I praise you because I am fearfully and wonderfully made; your works are wonderful, I know that full well." (New International Version) As you can see, David *knew* who he was. He knew he was special to God, even though the surrounding people tried to convince him otherwise. When people around David looked at him, they saw a young music-loving shepherd boy from the hills of Bethlehem. When God looked at David He saw a king.

Over nine hundred years after David, the Messiah arrived. He was a direct descendant of David. The man I am referring to is Jesus Christ. Jesus came into the world as an infant child. Despite who Jesus was, just like his ancestor David, Jesus didn't fit in. He was considered an outcast, a heretic, and was later put to death as a common criminal.

Many years before Christ, the prophet Isaiah foretold of the coming Messiah. Isaiah said, "My servant grew up in the Lord's presence like a tender green shoot, like a root in dry ground. There was nothing beautiful or majestic about his appearance, nothing to attract us to him. He was despised and rejected; a man of sorrows, acquainted with deepest grief. We turned our backs on him and looked the other way. He was despised, and we did not care." (Isaiah 53:2-3, New Living Translation)

Jesus died on the cross for our salvation and the world didn't even realize who he was. Jesus was rejected, mocked, beaten, and crucified. Just like his ancestor David, Jesus wasn't looking for someone to tell him he could be part of the club. He wasn't seeking the approval of those around him. Jesus knew his identity and his purpose. He knew this because he had been commissioned by God, his father. Though Jesus didn't fit in with the crowd, He was the greatest man that ever lived. Jesus didn't waste time attempting to be someone or something he was not.

I have learned many lessons since my days as an insecure kid with scoliosis struggling to fit in with the crowd. Now I see myself as God sees me and I know who I am in God. Find out who you are in God. You are special to God and He loves you! God has great plans for you. Discover what your purpose in life is from God. Unless you establish a personal relationship with God, you will not know your true identity and purpose. Not knowing your true identity and purpose will make you wander aimlessly. It will cause you to try to be something you weren't meant to be. Understanding your identity in God will give you a sense of direction and purpose. God will place people in your path that will allow you to fulfill the calling he has for your life.

God didn't create you to be like anyone else. Be thankful for the uniqueness that makes you who you are! You have unique gifts and talents in a mixture no one else has. Nobody can be you as effectively as you can! Don't seek to discover your identity, purpose, or potential, based on what others say or think about you. When you do that, you are trying to conform yourself to fit into the mold of what others expect from you. Romans 12:2 says, "Do not conform to the pattern of this world, but be transformed by the renewing of your mind. Then you will be able to test and approve what God's will is; his good, pleasing and perfect will." (New International Version)

If you want to reach your God-given potential and destiny, you must risk not fitting in. Not fitting in does not mean you are not loved, appreciated, and accepted. God loves you and will place people into your life who will love and accept you for who He called you to be. Why try to fit in when you were born to stand out?

LESSON # 2

DON'T EXPECT A TRAVEL ITINERARY

I've often thought life would be easier if we had a full travel itinerary for life from God. Nearly everyone can recall a time when they knew they couldn't stay in their current place or situation. Perhaps you are in one of those times in your life now. Life often requires difficult decisions. Major decisions would be easier if God gave us a full set of details telling us every move we should make.

It is a mistake to delay actions until you are 100% certain you are making the right decisions. Martin Luther King said, "Faith is taking the first step, even when we don't see the whole staircase." Often, God does not give us all the details. Too many people today are waiting for a sign or confirmation from God that their decisions are the right ones. Sometimes people say things to God such as, "God if you will cause this to happen, then I'll know it's you!" Have you ever played that game with God? This type of thinking has kept many from allowing God to lead them. They want God to post a sign on a billboard telling them what to do!

If you trust in God and commit yourself to him, he will lead you step by step. You must take the first step. Often, people want God to drop a detailed travel itinerary for life's journey in their lap. Think about your last flight itinerary from an airline you used. Your flight itinerary told you everything about your flight departure time, when and where it would stop, and the arrival time at your destination. That works for airline travel; it doesn't work in life. You don't get advance details about your journey through life.

In the 12th chapter of Genesis a story is found about a man named Abram, who God would later name Abraham. Abram was living in a place called Haran. God spoke to Abram and said, "I want you to move on from here." Take a look at the story in Genesis chapter 12.

"The Lord had said to Abram, 'Leave your native country, your relatives, and your father's family, and go to the land I will show you. I will make you into a great nation. I will bless you and make you famous, and you will be a blessing to others. I will bless those who bless you and curse those who treat you with contempt. All the families on earth will be blessed through you.' So, Abram departed as the Lord had instructed, and Lot (Abram's nephew), went with him." (Genesis 12:1-4, New Living Translation)

I see nowhere in the story that indicates that God told Abram *where* he was going. God only told Abram that He would *show* him. Abram didn't wait for a travel itinerary. It took faith by Abram to begin a journey, not knowing where his final destination would be. This journey changed his life and affected generations of people after him. A scripture in the Hebrews refers to this episode in Abram's life. Hebrews 11:8 says, *"It* was by faith that Abraham obeyed when God called him to leave home and go to another land that God would give him as his inheritance. He went without knowing where he was going." (New Living Translation)

Sometimes God directs people to begin a new chapter in their life, but He doesn't reveal all the details. God gives us information about his plans for our life in tiny bits and pieces.

I can somewhat relate to how Abram must have felt. In 2012, my wife Janet and I had a life changing and faith testing event occur in our lives. It involved a situation where God was directing our paths, but didn't give us as many of the details as we would have liked.

In the spring and early summer of 2012, Janet and I spent hours upon hours planning and coordinating our first mission trip. It was during August of that year we traveled from our home in St. Louis to a village in the rural mountains of Burundi, Africa. During that year, we were partnered with a missionary organization we had been introduced to through the church we were attending. The missionary organization ministered to the needs of orphaned and abandoned children in the village of Bukeye, Burundi.

Just for a quick geography lesson, Burundi is a tiny landlocked country in Central Africa. It is bordered by Rwanda to the North, Tanzania to the East and South, and The Democratic Republic of The Congo to the West. At the time of our visit, it ranked as the fifth poorest country in the world. It is on the list of *fourth* world countries. Before planning our trip, I had never heard of a fourth world country. Fourth world countries are the absolute poorest and least developed countries in the world.

Planning and preparing for our trip was stressful. We already had passports, but still needed travel visas, a written invitation from a sponsor within the country, emergency medical evacuation insurance, and immunizations for everything imaginable. We had to get hepatitis A shots, hepatitis B shots, tetanus shots, polio boosters, yellow fever shots, typhoid shots, and prescriptions for Malarone; an anti-malaria medication to take while we were there. By the time we finished getting the required shots, we were overwhelmed.

Two weeks before we were scheduled to fly to Burundi, something strange happened. On a Sunday morning while sitting in a worship service at the church where we were members, God spoke something to Janet that neither of us could have expected. It was a brief and distinct message from God to us we found alarming. Janet did not disclose what God had spoken to her until we walked out of church that morning. When we got into the car, Janet looked stunned. Janet said, "While we were in church, God told me I wasn't coming back." I can't remember what my first response was, but I was in a moment of shock. We had just spent the last several months doing extensive research on the land that God was calling us to visit. We had prayed and fasted for favor and had gone through loads of red tape to be cleared to travel to Burundi. Getting this message from God now was unexpected. The words that God spoke to Janet left us both dazed and confused.

In the following days, because of the message from God, we made a quick decision. We both hastily prepared a last will and testament document and had it notarized. Based on what we had heard from God, we didn't know whether either one of us would come back from Burundi. The worst-case scenarios flooded through our minds like a tidal wave. It might have been those thoughts that motivated us to buy emergency medical evacuation insurance. Despite God's strange message, we knew without a doubt God was calling us to spend nine days in the mountains of Burundi.

When the day to leave for Burundi finally arrived, we both felt a mixed variety of emotions. We were excited about experiencing our first mission trip. It allowed us to see a land and culture we had only read about for so long. Yet, there continued to be echoing reminders of what God had spoken to Janet, and those reminders brought us waves of uncertainty and fears of the unknown.

The journey to Burundi was a long and exhausting trip. Because of a 23 hour layover between connecting flights, we had to fly to Washington D.C. and spend the night. The next morning we boarded a plane to fly to Addis Ababa, Ethiopia. I had completely underestimated how tired we would be after spending 17 hours on a plane! After landing in Ethiopia, we boarded another plane for a 4 hour flight to Kigali, Rwanda. Finally, from Rwanda, we took a short commuter flight into

Don't Expect A Travel Itinerary

Bujumbura, Burundi.

When we arrived in Burundi where we would spend the next nine days, we were awestruck. We realized every mental image we had about Burundi was wrong. We had a preconceived idea Burundi would be a dry desert wasteland. It is quite the contrary. Burundi is a very mountainous country with beautiful rolling hills and lush vegetation. It is home to one of the largest and deepest fresh-water lakes in the world; Lake Tanganyika. Burundi is a beautiful country, but we also saw the heartbreaking side of Burundi. The level of poverty around us was intense. It was far worse than we could have imagined.

The missionary organization we were visiting in Burundi had built a children's village that included family based housing for orphaned and abandoned children. Plans were also in place to build a medical clinic in the children's village. Our time spent in Burundi proved to be a life changing experience for us. Janet and I ministered to the children and helped do landscaping around the children's homes. We had daily reminders that God's love and presence is everywhere throughout the world; not just in the local church back home.

When we returned home, we were physically and

emotionally depleted. We were still trying to digest and comprehend everything we had seen and done. I remember the first church service we attended at our church after returning home. That service felt strange and uncomfortable. It felt as if we were complete strangers in our own church. At first, we reasoned that we were both still exhausted from our trip, so we passed it off as nothing. The feelings of disconnection continued over the following month, but we weren't sure why.

During the following weeks, we had been discussing possible church Pastors we could contact about coming to their churches to speak as spokesmen in behalf of the missionary organization. One Sunday morning as I was lying in bed watching television in our bedroom, I caught a segment of a local church broadcast. This church was roughly 25 minutes from where we live. As I continued to watch the program, an attractive dark-haired woman came into the picture on the screen. She gave announcements about things taking place at their church. I called Janet into the room and told her, "I know this lady! I went to high school with her! We should go to that church to see if we can talk to her about our mission efforts in Burundi!" Janet agreed it was a good idea.

On the following Wednesday evening, we drove to visit the church we had seen on television that past Sunday morning. I still remember the exact date of our visit to the church. It was Wednesday October 10, 2012. As fate would have it, the former high school friend I had seen on the church broadcast was not at church that night. We stayed for the entire church service and loved the music, the sermon, and every other aspect of the church service.

After leaving and getting into our car, we looked at each other and read each other's minds. We had just experienced one of the most refreshing church services either of us had ever seen. What we received that night in church was ointment on our wounds. We discussed our experience that night and realized God had orchestrated and ordained our visit to the church. We knew we had found our new church home! Suddenly, we had a light bulb moment when what God had spoken to Janet weeks earlier made sense to us. We realized God was telling Janet she wasn't coming back to the *church* we had been attending.

Even though we tried to continue attending our former church, our hearts and minds were disengaged from the atmosphere in the church. We were trying to continue to make ourselves a part of somewhere we no longer belonged!

We made the church we visited our new church home, and we still attend there to this day. Looking back we both have to laugh. God could have been a little more specific when he told Janet, "You're not coming back." This proved to be a lesson to us that sometimes God will speak to you and be directing your steps, but he doesn't give you all the details. He is waiting for you to take a step of faith, and when you do, he will make his plan clear to you.

Now the question for you to consider is simple. Are you in a place in life where you feel God is leading you in a different direction? Just as in the situations with Abram, or with Janet and me, perhaps God is saying to you, "It's time to step out. Don't lean on your own understanding. Trust me." The thoughts and dreams that keep you awake at night aren't accidental. God speaks in a still small voice. He gives us small details at a time. He doesn't give us the whole travel itinerary.

If you want to reach your full potential and have a sense purpose for your life, sometimes you have to just get up and go. You can't sit and wait for God to drop a sign out of the sky. People often struggle through life trying to find true fulfillment and purpose. It is impossible to discover your true calling or purpose until you get up and get busy doing something! Volunteer at a hospital or a community shelter.

Go on a mission trip. Start the business you have dreamed of or write that book that has been burning within you! Perhaps you should teach that class you have been considering teaching at church. Why are you waiting?

When you trust God to lead you and take a step of faith, you will find your true purpose! You don't have to wait for a written message from God in the sky! In Psalm chapter 37 it says, "The Lord directs the steps of the godly. He delights in every detail of their lives. Though they stumble, they will never fall, for the Lord holds them by the hand." (Psalm 37-23-24, New Living Translation) This tells us God will direct our steps if we let him. He may not tell us our final destination, or give us a detailed travel itinerary right from the start, but He will guide us step by step. We have to start somewhere. God has a distinct plan and a purpose for your life. Step out in faith and God will fill you in little by little about what his plan is for you. Don't make the mistake of wasting years of your life waiting for God to give you a detailed travel itinerary.

LESSON # 3

SOMETIMES YOU MUST LET IT GO

You can't continue to hold things forever. Without laying items down you pick up, ability to function is soon lost. Your hands and arms become full, rendering them useless. Emotionally, socially, and spiritually people do that. Many fail to recognize what they need to lay aside.

Einstein once said the definition of insanity is doing the same things repeatedly and expecting different results. For personal and spiritual growth to occur, eventually we must change. Realizing what we need to release hold of in life is important. Harboring anger, bitterness, guilt, and regret will shipwreck your legacy. Your parents may not have left a great legacy. Maybe they were abusive, or struggled with addictions or major financial issues. The good news is dysfunctional lifestyles need not be a generational curse. Many emotional scars can result from a family history full of turmoil. Regardless of your family's past, you don't have to stay a victim. You can create a new legacy.

Creating a new legacy means choosing to be a victor instead of a victim. Because of a turbulent childhood, many people develop a victim mentality. People remember the painful segments of their childhood and continue embracing the pain. They reflect on past episodes of being misunderstood or neglected and never let go of the bitterness and anger. Ephesians 4:31-32 tells us, "Get rid of all bitterness, rage, anger, harsh words, and slander, as well as all types of evil behavior. Instead, be kind to each other, tenderhearted, forgiving one another, just as God through Christ has forgiven you." (New Living Translation) The words of the Apostle Paul here are very plain. Allowed to fester; bitterness, anger, hurts, and regrets will ruin your life. Do yourself a favor; let it go.

God can't place tomorrow's blessings in your hands if they are full of yesterday's junk. The pain and hurts from your past need to stay in the past where they belong. Today is a new day! You can't continue to carry your past hurts around like a piece of overfilled luggage. Have you ever packed too much luggage? If you have, you can remember how heavy your luggage was! Janet packs too much every time we travel! Heavy luggage causes you to struggle with the weight and bulkiness of it as you go through the airport. When you finally set your luggage down, you are relieved because you're exhausted. Life is like traveling. People often pack too much for life's journey. They go through life and continue to accumulate baggage from their past. The weight of their emotional baggage wears them out. If a person who has accumulated too much baggage in life ever sets it down, they will experience great relief and peace.

God has places He wants to take you and has a plan and purpose for your life. One of my favorite scriptures is Jeremiah 29:11. This scripture says, "For I know the plans I have for you, says the Lord. They are plans for good and not for disaster, to give you a future and a hope." (New Living Translation)

Are you laboring under the weight of past pain and hurts? Jesus said, "Come to me, all of you who are weary and carry heavy burdens, and I will give you rest." (Matthew 11:28, New Living Translation) When your arms are full of unnecessary baggage of your past, you stay too emotionally, mentally, and spiritually exhausted for God to lead you. During my life, there has been baggage I have set aside. Pain over broken relationships, mistakes, poor choices, and regret has tried to sneak into my luggage. Several times during my life, I've had to lighten my luggage. There are things God wanted me to keep packed. Others things have been a needless weight holding me back. I now travel light. When you carry around past defeats, you settle for a life of mediocrity that God never intended for you. You were created to be outstanding and to change lives. To become who God wants you to be, you may have to unpack.

My father often told of a lesson he had about letting go during his life. Dad was quite a character. I was the youngest of four children. My dad, born in 1919, was 44 by the time I was born. He was always an animated storyteller and often shared his life experiences. Sometimes Dad forgot which stories he already shared. Many of his experiences I heard told many times. One particular story he told never lost its luster.

As the story goes, in the summer of 1935, Dad had entered a local soapbox derby race held by Chevrolet Motor Company. After gathering what pieces of scrap lumber he could find, Dad began construction of his car. His dad (my grandfather) took a keen interest in what his 16-year-old son was building. My grandfather saw the project and told my dad, "Son, I'll help you build a winner!" My dad's father put 150 dollars into the project and got the help of his brother Bill, who owned a machine shop. Bill offered to machine the car parts. The completed soapbox racer had 20 inch wheels and maple axles. Another local boy in the neighborhood, Everett Miller, whose dad owned an auto repair shop, also entered the race. Everett's car had 20 inch wheels like my dad's car, but included an enclosed cockpit for the driver.

The series of races took place at St. Louis' Art Hill on a hot August day. By mid-afternoon, Everett and my dad had eliminated 500 cars from contention. A timekeeper told my dad that Everett's car having an enclosed cockpit made it slightly faster. Everett had also ground the sides of his tires for less contact with the pavement to gain more speed.

Dad's collection of spare parts included two extra tires as back-ups in case a blowout occurred. Because of the very warm summer temperatures and the ground down tires, Everett's car blew a tire. One of the race rulings stated that any car that couldn't be fixed in 15 minutes would be eliminated. When my dad heard the news about Everett's tire, he was ecstatic! Buying a replacement tire on a late Sunday afternoon would be almost impossible. Dad left to get a soda and sat enjoying the drink; gloating the whole time.

When Dad returned, he was surprised to see Everett got a tire. After one quick glance, Dad realized the spare on Everett's car was given to him by my grandfather. Dad was furious! He told his father, "You won't live long enough for me forgive you!" When the race resumed, Everett raced against my dad and eliminated him from further competition. The win ensured Everett the opportunity to travel to Akron, Ohio to race in the national competition.

When Everett returned from the nationals in Akron, he stopped by my dad's house to return the tire. Everett handed the tire to my grandfather and walked away. He never even said thank you for the tire. Everett's attitude made my dad even angrier.

Dad held onto an undercurrent of bitterness and anger toward his father for 20 years. In the autumn of 1955, Dad committed his life to Christ. God spoke to my dad and told him if he expected forgiveness of his sins, he needed to let it go and forgive his dad. Dad went to his father to forgive him and ask for his forgiveness, and they both cried. Dad set aside his baggage from the past and became a Christian. My dad's anger, resentment, and bitterness toward his father had sidetracked his God-given purpose for 20 years!

Think about your own life. What past bitterness, anger, or hurts are you holding onto that are keeping you from being happy? You can hold onto negativity and ill feelings from the past for so long, the feelings become the new normal. The hardest part of growing is letting go of the familiar and moving into territories unknown. Do you remember Abram's story? That's what he did. He moved on from what seemed normal into where God was leading. God doesn't want you to stay a prisoner of your past hurts and disappointments.

Consider for a moment the words of the famous *Serenity Prayer*. The three-part message in this prayer is powerful. First, the prayer asks God for peace to accept what can't be changed. You can put yourself through years of needless stress trying to change the unchangeable. You can't force others to change. Sometimes you can't avoid illness. Family struggles are often unavoidable. God can give you peace to accept what can't be changed. Stop expecting people and circumstances to be perfect. In doing so, you learn to appreciate them for who and what they are.

Second, the prayer asks God for courage to change what can be changed. It takes courage to change. When you change you are risking criticism. Change requires us to venture into the unknown. As long as you continue to do what you've done, you'll keep getting what you've got. You may have many painful memories and hurts from past events in your life. Moving on doesn't mean forgetting. It means choosing happiness over the pain.

One of my favorite Bible passages is found in Philippians 3:13-14. The Apostle Paul is quoted as saying, "Brothers and sisters I do not consider myself yet to have taken hold of it. But one thing I do: Forgetting what is behind and straining toward what is ahead, I press on toward the goal to win the prize for which God has called me heavenward in Christ Jesus." (New International Version) To paraphrase, Paul is saying. "I'm chasing my God-given destiny. I'm not fully there yet. But, I choose to forget the past and keep moving toward where God is leading me."

I discovered something interesting about the word "forgetting" as used in the passage. This scripture was originally written in Greek. The original Greek word for forget or forgetting is the word *epilanthanomai*. The word means to neglect or no longer care for something. Paul was saying he chose to not care about the past. Before his conversion to Christ, Paul was a ruthless, cold-hearted person. Paul still had memories of when he was stoning Christians before accepting Christ, but chose to not focus on those memories. Paul knew God had forgiven his past sins and mistakes. God has forgiven your sins of the past as well. You simply need to accept God's gift of Grace. The past cannot be changed. Your destiny and your legacy are still being written. Regardless of your past, you can still leave a legacy that is great.

Last, the Serenity Prayer asks God to give us wisdom to know the difference between what can and can't be changed. Far too many people waste years fighting a battle that isn't worth fighting. It is important to choose your battles wisely. This part of the Serenity Prayer is asking for wisdom. I believe everyone should ask God for wisdom. I love what James the brother of Christ said about asking for wisdom. James said, "If any of you lack wisdom, you should ask God, who gives generously to all without finding fault, and it will be given to you" (James 1:5, New International Version). The Bible also says in Proverbs 8:11, "For wisdom is far more valuable than rubies. Nothing you desire can compare with it." (New Living Translation)

I believe God is the only source of true wisdom. You can get a formal education, a college degree, and letters behind your name and you will have knowledge. Knowledge is wonderful, but it can't compare to wisdom. Knowledge is of little use without wisdom. Knowledge is a collection of facts and information about a situation. Wisdom equates to knowing how to apply the knowledge to better your life.

When I was young, my mother gave me a very simplistic explanation of knowledge versus wisdom. She said, "Knowledge is being aware the clock is broken, wisdom causes you to know how to fix it." Knowing a problem exists is one thing, knowing the steps to resolve the problem is another. Many people have knowledge of their problems in life but no wisdom to improve their circumstances. If you are facing a crisis in your life, ask God for wisdom. God will give you the wisdom to know what steps to take to lead you to your God-given destiny. Wisdom will help you know which battles to fight and which battles to let go.

What are your goals and dreams? Pray for God to show you his plan for your life. God can make your dreams become a reality if you commit yourself to him and trust him. Psalm 34: 4-5 tells us, "Take delight in the Lord, and he will give you your heart's desires. Commit everything you do to the Lord. Trust him, and he will help you." (New Living Translation)

You may need to lighten your luggage. Don't allow pain from your past to rob you of a great future. Use your past mistakes, failures, and hurts as guideposts, not hitching posts. Let go of your past and seek God's plan for your life. Your legacy is at stake; make it a great one.

LESSON # 4

ATTITUDE IS EVERYTHING

The *Merriam-Webster* dictionary defines attitude as a feeling or way of thinking that affects a person's behavior. I've learned the times I've struggled the most are when my feelings or thinking has soured. When I have allowed my attitudes about people and circumstances in life to become negative, I have felt defeated. My behavior during those times was toxic and reflected my attitudes.

You see the world through the filter of your attitude. How you see the world is governed by your attitudes and how you emotionally process your experiences in life. You may be unable to see the truth about your situation because of your attitude. Two people facing similar challenges can experience different degrees of success depending on their attitude. Your attitude will make you or break you. I love what the great motivational speaker and author Zig Ziglar said about attitude. He said, "Your attitude, not your aptitude, will determine your altitude." I believe that! You can never rise above the limitations of the attitudes you embrace.

Attitudes affect how you interact with others around you. Can you think of someone you know that oozes with negativity? You learn to never ask them how they are. They will tell you in depressing detail. These are the ones who fail to see the positive in their circumstances. Negative people always see the glass as half empty instead of half full.

Attitudes are contagious. I've learned to be very selective of the people I embrace as close friends. I try to treat everyone with love and respect, but I keep my circle of friends small. I want to be surrounded with positive and inspiring people. The quality of person you become is influenced by the company you keep. Enthusiasm and negativity are both contagious. Both can spread like a virus. Viruses are spread by contact with an infected human.

Scientists have discovered a single sneeze from a flu sufferer can infect an entire room. The contamination can last for hours. Negative attitudes and positive attitudes work the same way. Spend an hour with someone who spews negativity and you will be infected and leave feeling depressed. Spending time with a charismatic, upbeat person leaves you feeling encouraged and inspired.

Millions of people every year attend motivational seminars. They go hoping to be infected with hope. I love what my Pastor Daren Carstens says about attitude. Pastor Daren (affectionately known as PD) always says, "Christian people should be hope dealers." His catch phrase is "Attitude is everything!" Pastor Daren is right! Our attitudes should be positive enough to infect others with hope.

In relation to eternity, your life is very brief. The Bible says in James 4:14, "You do not even know what will happen tomorrow. What is your life? You are a mist that appears for a little while then vanishes." (New International Version) What James was saying is we get busy planning our future, but we're never guaranteed a tomorrow. Today is the day to begin creating a great legacy. Today you can make a positive impact on someone's life.

The scripture from James reminds me of something from my childhood. I remember times as a child when I had a bad cold. My mother would always prepare a warm mist vaporizer and place it by my bed, and the warm moist air always eased the congestion I had. Steam from the vaporizer worked to change the environment. The steam was visible then quickly disappeared. Even after the steam vanished, the moist air worked to improve the surrounding atmosphere. I once read that one of the most important things to remember about using a vaporizer is it must be kept clean. If not kept clean, bacteria will accumulate in the vaporizer and be vaporized into the air. This would contaminate the environment around the vaporizer, making it worse rather than better.

The same principle applies to your life. To offer an environment conducive to healing the hurting people around you, you have to stay clean in your thoughts, actions, and motives. You must allow God to transform your attitude so your life will offer healing to a hurting world. If you allow bitterness, strife, and envy to characterize your attitude, you will contaminate your environment. Your life is as a vapor. Like the vaporizer, the effects of the vapors of your life linger long after you are gone. The lingering vapor will be the legacy you leave. Are the vapors of your life conducive to healing or are they spreading toxins to those around you?

Negativity will cause you to develop a victim mentality. Someone once said, "A bad attitude is like a flat tire. If you don't change it, you won't go anywhere." A positive attitude will cause you to embrace hope. It will cause you to chase your dreams and accomplish your goals. Your attitudes play an enormous role in your destiny and the legacy you leave.

Your attitudes are constructed by the thoughts you embrace. Thoughts of inferiority, fear, guilt, shame, and bitterness will destroy you. Negative thoughts affect your attitudes, which affect your actions. I heard a quote that says, "Be careful of your thoughts, for your thoughts become words. Be careful of your words, for your words become actions. Be careful of your actions, for your actions become your habits. Be careful of your habits, for your habits become your character. Be careful of you character, for your character becomes your destiny."

Proverbs 4:23 says, "Guard your heart above all else, for it determines the course of your life." (New Living Translation) The word heart used in this scripture comes from the Hebrew word *leb*, meaning the feelings, will, and intellect. It is our feelings (emotions), will, and intellect that create our attitudes. Our thoughts produce our emotions and attitudes, which produce our actions. What this scripture is saying is "guard your thoughts." Your mind is like a battle ground. Much of your success in life comes from winning the battles and conquering the negative thoughts that invade your mind.

The Apostle Paul told the church in Philippi, "Do not be anxious about anything, but in every situation, by prayer and petition, present your requests to God. And the peace of God which transcends all understanding will guard your hearts and minds in Christ Jesus. Finally brothers and sisters, whatever is true, whatever is noble, whatever is right, whatever is pure, whatever is lovely, whatever is admirable,...if anything is excellent or praiseworthy...think on these things. (Philippians 4:6-8, New International Version)

You must make a conscious decision every day to guard your thoughts. Negativity, bitterness, hatred, and all other manner of junk continually fight for space in your mind. Someone with a great attitude looks beyond their dilemmas. They expect, believe, and visualize what they want to carry out. They see the sun behind every cloud and cling to hope in times of crisis. Those with great attitudes see problems as foes destined for defeat.

People with great attitudes are the encouragers, the motivators, and the folks everyone wishes they were. When a person with a great attitude enters a room, everyone knows they have arrived. The atmosphere of the room suddenly changes. They are the game-changers and mentors. Individuals with great attitudes cultivate their best strengths and extract the best from others. These upbeat folks help others see their own potential. This is the person God wants you to become.

I believe a person who strives to keep a great attitude is refusing a life of mediocrity. God isn't calling you to a life of mediocrity. Think of what the word mediocre means. The dictionary defines mediocre as "of only moderate quality; not very good." Synonyms for the word mediocre are words such as average, undistinguished, unexceptional, lackluster, and forgettable. Do these words describe how you want your life to be remembered? I seriously doubt they do. You want your life to be remembered as inspiring and exceptional. If you seek God's direction and plan for your life, he will lead and empower you to reach your full potential and inspire others.

Take one trip to an expensive but mediocre restaurant and you'd never want to go back. You wouldn't return because your experience would fall way short of your expectations. It would be an easily forgettable experience that you wouldn't want to replay. A great restaurant experience is memorable and creates a mindset that causes you to return. People often settle for being like the mediocre restaurant. What the menu of their life is serving and the service by which it is delivered is quickly forgettable. Their life isn't creating a positive mindset in the minds of others. Their life isn't offering anything with pizzazz. Making a difference requires *being* different. A life of mediocrity doesn't leave a great legacy.

To rise above mediocrity, you must have an outstanding attitude. Then, you can become the person God created you to be. That means discovering his plan for you and not trying to figure it out on our own. It means reading God's word and discovering what changes you need to make in your life. As you seek after God's will for your life, you transform. Your mindset, thoughts, and attitude transforms into what God wants for you. When that occurs, your actions reflect what your mind and attitude embraces, and you become a game-changer. It all starts with your attitude. If you settle for mediocrity that is all you will ever achieve. Mediocrity won't provide the encouragement, inspiration, and strength others around you desperately need.

Attitudes become actions and actions become habits. Habits mold, shape, and provide direction for your life. The habits and actions of your life become your destiny, which becomes your legacy. You surely want the best for those you love. What legacy do you want to leave them? Remember when it comes to your legacy, what matters is what you leave *in* them, not *to* them. What values are your attitudes and actions instilling in your loved ones? The best parting gift you can leave your friends and family is the legacy of a life lived being led by God and characterized by a great attitude. When your attitude is filtered through what God wants for you, your life will be positive and dynamic. It is that God-first life and attitude that will give you the abundant life Jesus spoke of in John 10:10. Examine your attitude. It is where your legacy begins.

LESSON # 5

LIFE BEGINS AT THE END OF YOUR COMFORT ZONE

Any goal or dream worth achieving in life requires a willingness to take a risk. This is a lesson I've learned and am continuing to learn. It is easy to become complacent in life and unwilling to venture into unfamiliar territory. Whether the unfamiliar territory involves new relationships, new careers, or major changes in habits or lifestyle, it all requires risk. Change requires risking criticism, failure, or being misunderstood.

Rather than take a risk, people often choose to stay with what is comfortable to them. We often hear the term "comfort zone" used. A person's comfort zone is created based upon things with which they are familiar or comfortable. The actions and the risks they are willing to take are governed by their comfort zone. Many people choose to never venture outside the limits of their comfort zone. I must admit in years past, I have been a prisoner of my comfort zone.

The problem with choosing to never leave your comfort zone is it prevents personal growth. The emotional, social, and spiritual growth we need requires a willingness to change, and change can be scary. Change often involves stepping into the unknown and taking a risk. Many of my greatest experiences and lessons in life came when I was stepping out and taking a chance. I believe a person robs themselves of life's greatest blessings if they stay a prisoner of their comfort zone. If we risk nothing, we do nothing. If we do nothing we will never become what God created us to be.

The comfort zone of a person is often created by fear. God doesn't want us to be afraid. The Bible tells us in 2nd Timothy 1:7, "For God has not given us a spirit of fear, but of power and of love and of a sound mind." (New King James Version) If our willingness to change is limited by fear, we aren't living by faith. Fear of failure, criticism, or rejection causes a person to resist action or change. When this happens, the comfort zone becomes a self-imposed prison and fear is the prison warden.

One of my earliest and most life-changing experiences of leaving my comfort zone occurred when I was 17. I was still a shy insecure teen, and an inmate of my comfort zone prison. One particular Wednesday evening, I was asked to speak to my church youth group. Public speaking was nowhere close to being on my "to do" list. Back then, I found public speaking terrifying. I spent a week preparing what to say and my talk lasted an agonizing 5 minutes. Those 5 minutes seemed like hours! It was so overwhelmingly scary for me I felt ill. Today, I can look back at that experience and laugh.

In the days that followed that experience, my mother occasionally allowed me to teach her Adult Sunday School class. In her wisdom and discernment, Mom saw a gift within me I didn't even see in myself. Public speaking continued to be unsettling, but it soon became easier. Eventually it became as natural as breathing. Since those days so long ago, I've taught many classes, led small groups, and facilitated workshops. Many of my most rewarding experiences have been while speaking to groups. I would have missed out on those rewarding experiences had I stayed trapped in my comfort zone. There is no price that can be placed on knowing your words have helped someone. Limiting God's work in our lives to the confines of our comfort zones robs us and others of potential blessings.

History would be different had great people of the past stayed within their comfort zones. Had the original disciples of Jesus remained paralyzed by fear, the early church would never have materialized. If Alexander Graham Bell had not risked failure, he would not have invented the telephone. What would life be like today if Albert Einstein, Thomas Edison, or Henry Ford had not used their gifts and taken a risk?

One great person who has changed the world is Billy Graham. Billy Graham has preached the Gospel to millions over the past 60 years. He has been credited with preaching to more people than anyone else in history! Imagine if he had been too afraid to preach his first sermon. If fear had kept him from his calling, millions of today's Christians may never have accepted Christ.

What you must realize is that being a prisoner of your comfort zone has widespread consequences. Your actions affect you and everyone around you. God created you to be an influential person of greatness. God never intended for you to live a life of mediocrity. There are works and purposes God wants you to fulfill. You have God-given gifts and talents waiting to be unleashed. Paul told Timothy to "Stir up the gift of God which is within you." People are waiting to be touched by your gift. You may not know the people, but they are waiting. They are waiting for you to become the person God has called you to be. Stepping out of your comfort zone to follow God's direction will change your life and the lives of those around you.

One of the most amazing accounts of a person stepping out of their comfort zone can be found in the Bible. The story is found in chapter 14 of the Gospel of Matthew. In the story, Jesus had just finished miraculously feeding 5000 people with 5 loaves of bread and 2 fish. This miracle occurred by the shores of the Sea of Galilee. After feeding the people, Jesus instructed his disciples to get in a boat and sail to the other shore. Jesus then went up into a mountain to pray.

In the very early hours of the morning before daylight, the disciples encountered very strong winds on the water. The wind was making rowing very difficult. As the storm grew worse, the waves became violent, and the disciples feared for their lives. At about 3:00 am, Jesus walked on the water toward the disciples in the boat. Because of the darkness, the disciples could barely see Jesus. They became afraid fearing it was a ghost. Then Jesus spoke to them saying, "It is me! Don't be afraid." When the disciples heard this, one disciple, Peter, became bold. Peter cried out to Jesus saying, "If it is you, command me to come to you on the water!" Jesus at once replied, "Come." Upon hearing Jesus, Peter stepped out of the boat onto the water.

This story reveals many truths. Peter's comfort zone quickly vanished when he heard the voice of Jesus. The boat which was his comfort zone became a vessel he wanted to vacate. Peter knew safety was no longer in the boat, but was where Jesus called him to be. Peter believed if he were to survive, he needed to follow the leading of Jesus. It required courage and faith on the part of Peter to leave the boat. To Peter, there were no guarantees he would survive, but he trusted Jesus. Peter wasn't relying on his own strength or abilities, but was relying on Jesus to take care of him.

When Peter hit the water, he walked as if he were on dry land. Peter was fine until his eyes left his destination, which was Jesus. Once Peter looked around and saw the waves, his confidence waned and he was relying on his own abilities. Peter became afraid and started sinking. Immediately, Peter cried out to Jesus and said, "Lord, save me!" At that moment, Jesus reached down and pulled Peter up and led him to the boat. As soon as they entered the boat, the winds stopped. The disciples then worshipped Jesus and said, "Truly you are the Son of God."

Peter's boldness and willingness to leave his comfort zone

of the boat affected him and the others. All the disciples saw the miracle. Just as Peter in the boat, you may realize that you need to step out. You know you cannot continue to play it safe in your comfort zone because Jesus is calling you. The confines of your comfort zone actually provide no safety at all. He is calling you to have faith. Jesus is calling you to depend upon him and not rely on your own abilities or even what seems logical. In Proverbs 3:5-6 the Bible says, "Trust in the Lord with all your heart; do not depend on your own understanding. Seek his will in all you do and he will show you which paths to take." (New Living Translation)

God has places he wants to lead you to in life. You will never reach your God-given potential if you stay in the boat. You can't worry about the waves of fear, criticism, or rejection you risk facing. Don't look at the waves. Look at Jesus. Jesus will never call you to a place and allow you to drown. You may not feel qualified to do what God is calling you to do. In yourself, you aren't qualified. The good news is God doesn't call the qualified, he qualifies the called. If you will submit yourself to God and be willing to leave your comfort zone, God will direct your paths. Remember the words of the Apostle Paul when he said, "I can do all things through Christ who strengthens me." (Philippians 4:13)

If you have read this book this far, I know you want to be everything God created you to be. Getting to that place in life requires you to trust God. It is time for you to ask yourself, "What makes up the comfort zone that holds me back? In what ways do I need to trust God more?" God may have a life-changing experience or journey in store for you, but you have to get out of the boat. I believe your greatest days begin when you let go of the constraints of your comfort zone. You have the potential for greatness. Someone once said, "Ships are safe in the harbor, but that is not what ships are for." It may be time for you to cut the ropes keeping you in the harbor and sail toward your destiny. When you leave the waters of your comfort zone, life truly begins.

LESSON #6

WE HAVE PLENTY TO OFFER GOD

My most difficult lesson has been learning to see myself as God sees me. As a kid, I always looked at myself as second-rate. I didn't feel smart enough, talented enough, or good enough. Being raised in a very legalistic church environment didn't help. The church of my childhood focused strongly on appearances and outward shows of "holiness." There were many implied rules for "Godly living." Teaching focused on the man-made rules to become acceptable to God. The message being served was I needed to earn God's acceptance.

Until I reached my early thirties, I didn't fully understand God's grace. The word grace means unmerited favor. God's grace cannot be earned; it is a gift. If earning it were possible, Jesus dying on the cross would have been unnecessary. Jesus paid the price necessary for our salvation. This reminds me of an old song that used to be sung in church. The song said, "He (Jesus) paid a debt he did not owe, I owed a debt I could not pay. I needed someone to wash my sins away." The debt that Jesus paid on the cross was one mankind could not pay. The cross was a picture of God's grace.

Even after becoming a Christian, I wondered how I could be good enough *for* God. I had it all wrong. It is *through* God we are made righteous. 2nd Corinthians 5:21 says, "For God made Christ, who never sinned, to be the offering for our sin, so that we could be made right with God *through* Christ." (New Living Translation) Without Christ, we can never offer God enough. But through Christ, we have plenty to offer God. God takes what we offer him, blesses it, and multiplies it. God wants to use us to bless others. This requires us to offer what we have to God and allow him to bless and multiply it. A story found in the 6th chapter of John's gospel illustrates this principle.

In the story from John chapter 6, Jesus had withdrawn by boat to a private place. When the people around town heard of this, massive crowds followed him. The crowds followed him because they had seen him heal the sick.

The story from John chapter 6 verses 5-13 is as follows:

When Jesus looked up and saw a great crowd coming toward him, he said to Philip, "Where shall we buy bread for these people to eat?"

He asked this only to test him, for he already had in mind what he was going to do. Philip answered him, "It would take more than half a year's wages to buy enough bread for each one to have a bite!"

Another of his disciples, Andrew, Simon Peter's brother, spoke up, "Here is a boy with five small barley loaves and two small fish, but how far will they go among so many?"

Jesus said, "Have the people sit down." There was plenty of grass in that place, and they sat down (about five thousand men were there). Jesus then took the loaves, gave thanks, and distributed to those who were seated as much as they wanted. He did the same with the fish.

When they had all had enough to eat, he said to his disciples, "Gather the pieces that are left over. Let nothing be wasted." So, they gathered them and filled twelve baskets with the pieces of the five barley loaves left over by those who had eaten. (New International Version)

Consider the scene in this story. An enormous crowd followed Jesus to this place. The people followed him because of hearing of him healing the sick. They wanted to witness and experience the supernatural. Daylight was fading, and the people were tired and hungry. There were over 5000 people surrounding Jesus and the disciples. Upon seeing the hungry crowd, Jesus sprung into action. He asked one of his disciples, Philip, "Where are we going to buy bread to feed these people?" Actually, Jesus already had a plan in place. He simply wanted to test the disciples' faith. Philip acknowledged they didn't have the money to buy enough food.

Another disciple, Andrew, brought a young boy from the crowd forward. The boy had 5 loaves of bread and two fish. Andrew saw what the boy offered and immediately doubted. He reasoned that the food delivery would run out very quickly. Andrew was thinking in the natural. Jesus operates in the supernatural. I once heard someone say "God puts his super on our natural."

Throughout the years, I have heard this story used in many sermons. But, I've rarely heard it shared focusing on the boy's perspective. My imagination runs wild with this story. I can imagine maybe his mother sent him grocery shopping. He may have been on his way home with the food when he wandered into the crowd. When asked, the boy offered what food he had to Jesus. The young lad took a step of faith. Maybe for a second he wondered what his mother would say if he returned home with no food. Would she be angry because he gave the groceries away? Now, I realize the Bible suggests none of this. This is just my imagination talking.

As soon as Jesus took the bread and fish, He blessed it and passed it among the people. Nothing in the story indicates that Jesus prayed for more food. He only blessed what was offered. After all the people had eaten, Jesus instructed his disciples to collect the leftovers. By this point, I'm certain the disciples were astonished. What seemed an insignificant amount of food continued to multiply. It fed the entire crowd, with plenty to spare! Had the boy distributed the food himself, the supply would have vanished quickly. It was offering it to Jesus that set the miracle into motion. When collected, the leftovers filled twelve baskets!

I have often heard it suggested there was one basket left for each disciple. I prefer to believe the spoils went to the boy. The food remaining exceeded what he originally had. It reminds me of the words of Jesus in Luke 6:38. In this passage, Jesus said, "Give and it will be given to you. A good measure, pressed down, shaken together and running over, will be poured into your lap. For with the measure you use, it will be measured to you." The boy gave everything he had. It was returned to him in abundance.

Now allow me to apply this to your life today. Multitudes

of people around you are hungry. They are hungry for peace in their life, a sense of purpose, happiness, and an experience with Christ. People around you are waiting for you to share what you have. There are talents, gifts, strengths, and callings within you. Keeping what you have to yourself will leave people hungry. Also, if you try to share what you have without giving it to Christ, it won't be enough to make an impact. God created you to make a difference in the lives of others. What you offer Jesus may seem insignificant to you or those around you. People have a tendency to look at the substance of your gift rather than the potential of your gift. God takes the ordinary and does the extraordinary.

In the story of the loaves and fish, the boy gave it to Jesus. When the boy turned over his food, he may not have realized Jesus was God in the flesh. The boy gave what he had to the Creator. He who hung the stars and created the sun was holding what the boy offered. God himself was in control of the boy's gift. The miracle displayed Jesus' ability to provide, and the disciples saw the miracle up close. I would guess they shared the story of that day many times. It was a life changing experience for them. The miraculous event affected the lives of thousands of people, and it all started with one boy. One boy's willingness to offer what little he had to Jesus affected thousands of people. The ripple effect of his faith and generosity changed lives forever.

You must be willing to give what you have to God. In the past I've attempted to work *for* God. What I've learned is I must work *through* God. Work done apart from God's blessing will never be enough. But, when you offer yourself and your gifts to God, He multiplies it abundantly. Miraculous things can then happen and lives can be changed. The Bible doesn't say we can do all things *for* God who strengthens us. It says was can do all things *through* God who strengthens us. (Philippians 4:13) Regardless of how small or insignificant your gift may seem, God can use it. If you are to become the person God created you to be, you must offer what you have to him.

God created mankind in his likeness and his image. The characteristics of God are in you. They may lie dormant, but they are there. You have the potential within you to live a life that mirrors God's image. You may not be exhibiting the fullness of the potential God placed within you, but that potential is there. For example, God is the epitome of love. The Bible tells us God *is* love. Because God is love, and we were created in his image, we have potential and ability to love. But, love in the truest sense is impossible apart from God. Look at what 1 John Chapter 4 says. This passage of scripture tells us, "Beloved, let us love one another, for love is from God; and whoever loves is born of God and knows God. Anyone who does not love does not know God, because God is love." (1 John 4:7-8, English Standard Version)

Another attribute of God that dwells within us is creativity. Because God is the Creator, we have a capacity and desire to create. We have the potential to make things. Artists make paintings and sculptures. Writers create through the books they write. Musicians make beautiful music. Seamstresses create garments. Carpenters build homes and other buildings. The potential for creativity came from God.

You have the potential to exhibit the characteristics of God in your life. That potential is there because you were created in God's image with the capacity for greatness. To leave a great legacy, you must offer the gifts and talents that God placed within you back to God. Allow him to use the talents and potential he placed within you. In doing so, you can become all that God created you to be. I once heard a quote that said, "What we are is God's gift to us. What we become is our gift to God."

Now it is time for you to reflect. What do you offer God?

Never underestimate what God can do with your gifts. Life changing gifts and potential dwell within you. You have to share your gifts and allow God to bless them. You may think what you offer is insufficient. Through your own efforts, your gifts are insufficient. With God's blessings, your gifts will multiply to change the world. You have plenty to offer God.

LESSON # 7

DEBT IS A PRISON

I wish someone had warned me earlier of the hazards of debt. Though debt is stressful, it has taught me many valuable lessons. I almost view the word debt as profanity. Debt is a four letter word. Much of the stress I have experienced resulted from debt. Financial struggles brought on by debt are one of the leading causes of stress in families today. Debt becomes a self-imposed prison. It places you into a prison of stress and anxiety that need not be a part of your life.

Patience has never been one of my strongest virtues. In the past, my impatience combined with my insecurity and low self-esteem was a recipe for disaster. I wanted "stuff" and I wanted it now. Using credit cards to buy things I couldn't actually afford became my standard practice. I bought things I couldn't afford and didn't need, with money I didn't have. I was trying to impress people who didn't care. My past tendencies toward materialism placed my life in turmoil. There was a time Janet and I had enough credit cards to shuffle like playing cards. Our level of debt was a runaway train headed for bankruptcy.

I can still remember the past credit accounts we held simultaneously. Our credit cards included Macy's, Kohl's, JC Penny, Discover, Lowe's, Best Buy, Capital One, Bank of America, Citibank, and a credit union Visa. We also had an outstanding 401k loan, a credit union line of credit, two auto loans, and our mortgage. We were in a prison of debt with no hope for parole.

During our deepest debt, Janet became inspired to start her own business. She had been working as a medical recruiter at a St. Louis based firm for years. When the ownership of that firm changed hands, the company's ethics deteriorated dramatically. The company no longer cared about ethical business practices. Therefore, Janet decided she could not continue to represent the company and stay in that environment.

Due to a non-compete clause in her employment contract, Janet had to work outside the medical recruiting industry for one year. After the one-year period ended in 2009, Janet wrote a business plan and called various banks to get a small business loan. Janet called seven different financial institutions and was rejected seven times. It wasn't surprising. Our credit history was horrific. Both Janet and I believed God was leading her into entrepreneurship. But, it was becoming obvious borrowing money to start a business wasn't what God had in mind.

At the same time we were trying to get the business started, we were also attempting to attack our debt crisis. I will never forget the day Janet spent an hour on the phone with a consumer credit counseling agency. The woman she spoke to asked for information regarding our sources of income. She then wanted to know the outstanding balances on our credit accounts. After evaluating our financial situation, what she told Janet served as a wake-up call to us. She said, "Janet, My job is to develop a systematic plan to help people repay their debt. Your income to debt ratio is very imbalanced. I rarely recommend bankruptcy, but based on your situation, that is your best choice."

We were devastated. What we feared was coming was suggested to us as our best choice. As much as it seemed the most logical option, we couldn't accept that as our plan. We believed in our hearts there was a better way. Immediately we began to pray and ask God for direction. We knew God didn't lead us to step out in faith only to abandon us.

Shortly thereafter, we stumbled upon material written by financial expert and author Dave Ramsey. We were intrigued by his plan for eliminating debt. The fact that he is a devout Christian also appealed to us. We began to implement the principles that Dave teaches and it changed our life. After using Dave Ramsey's methods for nearly a year, we discovered his in-class program *Financial Peace University*™. We decided to enroll in a class being offered at our church and it proved to be one of the best decisions we've ever made. We were helped so much by the class we chose to begin leading the class ourselves. We wanted to share what we had learned with others who were in debt. If you are seeking a system or plan to eliminate debt, I highly recommend *Financial Peace University*™.

With a trust in God and little money, we took a step of faith and started Janet's business. On June 8, 2009, Cornerstone Medical Recruiting was founded. We chose the name Cornerstone because of the scripture found in Ephesians 2:20 that refers to Jesus as the Chief Cornerstone. The company we started is built upon our faith and trust in Jesus himself. We never got a small business loan. As I write this, our business is 7 years old and still debt free. God is such an awesome God! We could not have accomplished what we did without God's leading, wisdom, and provision.

The first few months were scary, but God provided all of our needs.

Our financial situation has improved immensely since hearing the bankruptcy suggestion from the consumer credit counseling woman. I've learned no amount of material possessions can give you happiness. Never borrow money and expect to buy contentment. Eventually the newness of your purchases fade, you're stuck with debt, and still not happy. The only true source of happiness comes from a relationship with Jesus Christ. The human spirit has a vacancy only Jesus can fill. No amount of money or possessions can fill that void. I'm so thankful I came to that realization. Learning that lesson delivered me from my materialistic, credit card swiping ways. After promising each other we would never use credit again, Janet and I paid off approximately 80,000 dollars of junk debt. At the time of this writing, Janet and I are debt free except for our mortgage, which will be paid off in the next five years.

Over the years, Janet and I discovered the Bible has a tremendous amount to say about money. Jesus apparently thought money was an important topic because it was the topic of nearly half of Jesus' parables. The Bible has 500 verses about prayer, less than 500 verses about faith, and more than 2,000 verses about money. Jesus taught more about money than he taught on Heaven and Hell combined.

The Bible gives us clear direction about what is and is not morally acceptable. It also gives us advice about which actions are wise and which actions are foolish. Nowhere in the Bible does it suggest debt is a sin. But, the Bible strongly advises against debt. The Bible makes it clear that accumulating debt is foolish. One of the primary scriptures of the Bible that warns against debt is found in Proverbs. Proverbs 22:7 says, "The rich rule over the poor, and the borrower is slave to the lender." (New International Version) Debt takes away your freedom. You become a prisoner of stress and anxiety brought on by your indebtedness.

I now realize my debt was brought on by materialism. My thirst for possessions comparable to my friends led to borrowing money. I was trying to keep up appearances of success. There is nothing wrong with having nice material possessions. The problem arises when our possessions have us. Jesus once asked his disciples, "What does it profit a man to gain the whole world and lose his soul?"

When we allow ourselves to become focused on obtaining "things", the things become what we worship. The

Bible says in Matthew 6:19-21, "Do not store up for yourselves treasures on earth, where moths and vermin destroy, and where thieves break in and steal. But, store up for yourselves treasures in Heaven, where moths and vermin do not destroy, and thieves do not break in and steal. For where your treasure is, there your heart will be also." (New International Version) What a person does with their money and possessions reveal their true priorities. If your money and passions become your treasure, you'll never have a heart that seeks God's will for your life.

Today I understand everything I have belongs to God. My possessions and money are under my stewardship, but God is the owner. You must come to understand you are a steward, not an owner. A steward is one who manages the property of another. The Psalmist David said, "The earth is the Lord's and everything in it. The world and all the people belong to him." That makes it clear God owns everything.

Our money and possessions have been borrowed from God. I remember a song an elderly couple I knew often sang in church. The song was entitled, "Remind Me Dear Lord." The words of the song said:
The things that I love
and hold dear to my heart

are just borrowed,

they're not mine at all.

Jesus only let me use them

to brighten my life.

So remind me, remind me dear Lord.

Roll back the curtains of memory now and then.

Show me where you brought me from,

and where I could have been.

Remember I'm human and humans forget.

So remind me, remind me dear Lord.

The words of that song still ring true. Everything we have is borrowed from God. We are blessed by God to be a blessing. We must remember what God has done for us, and the place from which he has brought us.

When you come to understand stewardship, your priorities change. Your focus shifts away from using your money and possessions for selfish reasons. You then use what God has given you to honor him. Major amounts of debt keep us from doing God's work.

When I look back on my days of being in debt, I have to wonder about missed opportunities. How many opportunities to support God's work did I miss because I was broke? Broke people don't support charities, build water wells in third world countries, or give generously to their local church. Consider what you could do for the Kingdom of God if you had no debt! Not being a good steward of what God has given us robs God and us. It prohibits us from being able to sow seed into God's Kingdom. Janet and I have discovered no joy compares to the joy of giving. The joy of knowing financial seed that has been sown is making a difference in the lives of others is priceless. When all of your seed is going to pay loan payments and interest on debt, you're missing out. You are missing out on one of life's greatest joys; being a good steward of God's money.

Your stewardship plays a vital role in determining the blessings you experience, and your capacity to bless others. The degree to which you have blessed others and positively affected their life will determine the legacy you leave. When you live a life overwhelmed by debt, you are not exercising good stewardship. God has entrusted you with money, possessions, talents, and gifts. You have been entrusted with much. Luke 12:48 tells us, "When someone has been given much, much will be required in return; and when someone has been entrusted with much, even more will be required." (New Living Translation)

I am very thankful my wife and I were shaken by God and made to realize we were not being good stewards. God has tremendous plans for your life and blessings waiting for you. Living under the tension and stress of debt causes you to lose focus of God's purposes and plans for your life. Ask God to help you to become a good steward of the things he has entrusted to you. If you are in debt, begin a plan to become debt free. Escaping the prison of debt will help propel you to becoming everything God called you to be.

LESSON # 8

RELIGION IS A TRAP

Over the past 30 years I have come to love Jesus but despise religion. I grew up in church environments that oozed with religion. Before I go any further, allow me to give you my definition of religion. Religion is basically man-made rules to get to God. Religion is about trying to gain God's approval through improved behavior and lifestyles. Religion focuses more on the outward appearances rather than an inward transformation.

I consider myself blessed to have been raised by two devout Christian parents. My parents were careful in making sure I was taught biblical principals from a young age. I am thankful for my Christian heritage. During my years growing up, I was part of a conservative mainline Protestant church denomination. The church I grew up in had sound biblical teaching, but placed too much emphasis on rules and tradition. Allow me a few moments to explain.

In the church of my childhood, it was made clear to the members what the expected "rules" were. There were expectations of conduct that were politely forced upon members of the church. Church tradition and implied rules attempted to regulate the lifestyle of the members. For instance, I was told from a young age it was wrong to go to any business establishment that sold alcoholic beverages. This made the skating rink, bowling alleys, or restaurants that served alcohol off limits. The men were expected to wear white dress shirts and keep their hair cut short. The women were expected to not wear slacks and wear little to no jewelry or makeup. I can still remember the altar benches at the front of the church. Almost every church service ended with the minister inviting people to come pray at the altar. This became known as the "altar call." Often people would go to the altar to pray and accept the invitation to become a Christian. Sadly, far too often those who had just become Christians were quickly whisked away after praying to be informed of the "rules." They were quickly advised what they couldn't do as Christians. The whole environment reeked of religion.

When I think of religion, I think of the Pharisees. In the days of Jesus' ministry, the Pharisees were the Jewish religious leaders. They believed that pleasing God required meticulously adhering to a long list of religious rules and regulations. The foundation of these rules was the Mosaic

Law. God gave the Law through Moses to the Jewish people of the Old Testament. The most notable part of the Mosaic Law is the Ten Commandments, but they represented only 10 of the 613 commandments given to the Jewish people. As if obeying 613 laws wasn't difficult enough, the Pharisees gradually added to these laws. In their attempts to clarify the original laws, they ended up adding layers of complicated regulations. So for the Pharisees, they not only tried to live according to the original 613 laws, but also according to thousands of added laws. The Pharisees prided themselves in not only following God's written laws, but also the laws they themselves created. Jesus criticized the Pharisees for being legalistic and not focusing on true love for God and man.

Take a look at what Jesus said to the Pharisees in the 23rd chapter of Matthew:

"What sorrow awaits you teachers of religious law and you Pharisees; hypocrites! You are careful to tithe even the tiniest income from your herb gardens, but you ignore the more important aspects of the law; justice, mercy and faith. You should tithes, yes, but do not neglect the more important things. Blind guides, you strain your water so you won't accidently swallow a gnat, but you swallow a camel! What sorrow awaits you teachers of religious law and you Pharisees; hypocrites! You are careful to clean the outside of the cup and the dish, but inside you are filthy; full of greed and indulgence! First, wash the inside of the cup and the dish, and then the outside will become clean too. What sorrow awaits you teachers of religious law and you Pharisees; hypocrites! You are like whitewashed tombs; beautiful on the outside, but filled on the inside with dead people's bones and all sorts of impurity. Outwardly you look like righteous people, but inwardly you hearts are filled with hypocrisy and lawlessness." (Matthew 23:23-27, New Living Translation)

Those were strong words from Jesus to the Pharisees. Jesus was telling them they were so caught up in legalism they neglected the important things. Their strong focus on outward shows of religious behavior replaced a lifestyle that would have pleased God. Jesus told them that if they would focus on getting their hearts right with God, the outward expressions of their faith would take care of itself. Much can be learned from this. Jesus was popular with the sinners, but unpopular with the religious crowd. Think about that for a moment! The religious rules and regulations of the Pharisees did nothing to make them acceptable to God. Their legalism did nothing but place them in bondage of religion.

God didn't send Jesus into this world to enforce religion. Jesus was sent into the world to restore man's broken relationship with God. Religion tries to set guidelines to earn God's favor based on what we do. In reality, our favor with God is based on what Jesus did on the cross. I love how the New Living Bible version expresses a verse found in Ephesians 2:8. That scripture says, "God saved you by his grace when you believed, and you can't take credit for this; it is a gift from God." The word grace means unmerited favor. It is favor from God we don't deserve. God's grace can't be earned. It can only be freely received. Eternal life through Jesus Christ is God's gift to us.

You can't earn a gift. When you earn something, it is not a gift; it is your wage. Your wage is based on what you do. When all mankind was imprisoned by sin, God sent Jesus to die as the supreme sacrifice for our sins. Mankind couldn't earn what Jesus did. Romans 6:23 tells us, "For the wages of sin is death, but the gift of God is eternal life through Jesus Christ our Lord." (New International Version) Religion attempts to make God's gift a wage. Religion suggests that salvation from God is based on our behavior. Only a life transformed by God's grace will produce actions pleasing to God. The price needed to purchase our salvation was a price mankind couldn't pay. It was for this reason Jesus paid the price for us. God's intent was to offer salvation as a gift, and only through a relationship with Christ can we receive it.

Religion places people in a trap. Until I understood God's grace, I never felt good enough. I tried my best to live up to the rules and regulations of religion I had been taught, but always failed. The peace of God that passes all understanding continued to elude me. What I eventually learned is that nothing I could do would give me the peace I was seeking. Regardless of how hard I tried to measure up, the guilt and shame of my past remained. I was trying to make myself worthy through my actions, which was impossible. I didn't realize Jesus had already done everything necessary to make me acceptable to God. I simply needed to accept God's gift of grace.

The main reason religion doesn't work is that it teaches people to attempt the impossible. Religion teaches people to try harder to live a life pleasing to God. Religion can change a person's behavior, but it fails to change the person. Only God can transform a life into a life pleasing to God. Becoming what God created you to be begins internally, not externally. Church attendance is great, but church attendance alone won't put you into a right relationship with God. No amount of money given to the church or church songs sung while there can give you peace with God. Only a relationship with Christ and accepting the gift of God's grace can do that. When you try to follow a list of rules and regulations to receive peace with God, you will fail every time. The rules and regulations will keep you trapped in something God never designed; religion.

Religion traps people by causing them to be deceived. Religion often causes people to become self-righteous, thinking that their lifestyle and good behavior is enough. A passage of scripture in the Gospel of Matthew addresses this issue. The 19th chapter of the Gospel of Matthew has a story of a rich young ruler who came to Jesus with a question. Take a look at the story.

Someone came to Jesus with this question: "Teacher, what good deed must I do to have eternal life?" "Why ask me about what is good?" Jesus replied. "There is only one who is good. But to answer your question—if you want to receive eternal life, keep the commandments."

"Which ones?" the man asked.

Jesus replied, "You must not murder. You must not commit adultery. You must not steal. You must not testify falsely. Honor your father and mother. Love your neighbor as yourself."

"I've obeyed all these commandments," the young man replied. "What else must I do?"

Jesus told him, "If you want to be perfect, go and sell all your possessions and give the money to the poor, and you will have treasure in heaven. Then come, follow me."

But when the young man heard this, he went away sad, for he had many possessions. (Matthew 19:16-22, New Living Translation)

The young man was trapped in religion. He believed there was some good deed he may have missed that was keeping him from eternal life. The young man became confused when Jesus reviewed the commandments for him. He knew something was missing. He told Jesus he had followed all the commandments Jesus mentioned. Then Jesus told the young man to go sell his possessions and give the money to the poor. Upon hearing this, the young man was sad because he could not part with his money.

During this conversation, Jesus was testing the young man. Jesus was making the man aware of the condition of his heart. Only an encounter with Jesus can make a person aware of their spiritual condition. Religion can't do that. The young man lived by the commandments, but he wasn't changed by them. The young man treasured his money and possessions.

In Matthew 6:19-21, Jesus said, "Do not store up for

yourselves treasures on earth, where moths and vermin destroy, and where thieves break in and steal. But store up for yourselves treasures in heaven, where moths and vermin do not destroy, and where thieves do not break in and steal. For where your treasure is, there your heart will be also." (New International Version) The young man's treasure was in his wealth. Because that was where his treasure was, his heart was also there. There is nothing wrong with having wealth as long as your wealth doesn't have you.

What the young man lacked was a commitment to Jesus. His commitment was to religion and his wealth. Religion never places a person into a proper relationship with God. People often get it backwards. You can't follow God's commandments to develop a right standing with God. You have to develop a right standing with God so you *can* follow his commandments. Following the commandments alone doesn't justify a person in God's sight. In yourself, you can do nothing to please God. It is only through his power and grace you can live a life that pleases him. When Jesus is your treasure, your heart will be focused on living a life that pleases God.

Placing faith in religion and rules to earn favor with God is futile. Don't allow yourself to fall into that trap. The enemy of your soul, Satan, wants you to be focused on legalism and religion. He knows religion will not free you from the bondage of sin, but Jesus will. One of the most famous scriptures in the Bible says everything we need to know about having a right standing with God. That scripture is John 3:16. The scripture says, "For God loved the world so much that he gave his one and only Son, so that anyone who believes in him will not perish but have eternal life." (New Living Translation) You only have to believe and receive what God has done for you. When you accept God's grace and forgiveness, your life will never be the same. Living according to his commands won't be a struggle then; it will be a joy. Peace with God is something religion can never offer.

LESSON # 9

HAPPINESS IS A CHOICE

The idea that happiness is a choice was constantly voiced by my mother when I was a child. I often heard her express the idea but I never truly understood it until I was a grown man. I eventually realized my mother was right and that her words spoke wisdom. As cliché or simplistic as it may sound, it is true. Happiness is without a doubt a choice.

I spent many years of my childhood and early adulthood seeking happiness. The harder I searched for happiness the more frustrated I became. Like many others, I reasoned when I became wealthy enough, I'd be happy. Sometimes I thought when I acquired the right job, I'd be happy. For years, I thought I needed specific conditions to be happy.

After spending many years seeking happiness from the wrong sources, I became emotionally depleted. I am not sure exactly when it happened, but I finally understood my mother's words. Her words of wisdom rang in my ears. It was then I decided to live life and be happy. I came to the realization that I was basing my happiness on things beyond my control. When I chose to base my happiness on those things I *can* control, I felt empowered.

The problem with basing happiness on your circumstances is that circumstances continually change. Your job situation and income can change. Relationships with the people around you can change. Your health can change. The list of changes that can take place in life is endless. Circumstances are subject to change. If you depend on particular circumstances for happiness, and the situations change, you can suddenly lose your happiness.

I now understand that I can base my happiness on two unchangeable facts. The first unchangeable fact is we as humans have the God-given ability of choice. You can choose how you view and react to your circumstances. The second unchangeable fact is there is a God who loves us that never changes. God loved you enough to send his own son to die in your place. Through the sacrifice of Jesus, God's son, you can have eternal life. You don't have to spend your natural life in turmoil and eternity in Hell. That fact alone should make you happy!

You can decide to take control of your attitudes and responses to your circumstances. You can also consciously decide to put your faith in a loving and unchanging God. Apart from God, it is impossible to have true happiness. You can never live life to the fullest apart from God. To fully understand this from a biblical aspect, you need to read the 15th chapter of John's Gospel. Apart from God we can do nothing. In that chapter Jesus said, "As the Father has loved me, so have I loved you. Now remain in my love. If you keep my commands, you will remain in my love, just as I have kept my Father's commands and remain in his love. I have told you this so that my joy may be in you and that your joy may be complete." (John 15:9-11, New International Version)

In scripture, Jesus referred to Satan, the enemy of our souls, as a thief. In the 10th chapter of the Gospel of John Jesus said, "The thief comes only to steal and kill and destroy; I have come that they may have life, and have it to the full." Satan wants us to stay in distress, turmoil, and a state of unhappiness. Jesus died for us that we may have life and live it to the fullest.

What your attitudes will be throughout life and whether you place faith in God is based on choices you make. It is choices, not circumstances that bring about happiness. You can choose to focus on the positive aspects of your life rather than the negative. You can also choose to not be distracted by the constantly changing circumstances around you. Proverbs 3:5 tells us to trust God with all of our hearts and to not lean unto our own understanding. You don't have to understand why you are facing the circumstances you face. You only need to have faith and trust God; knowing He has a plan for your life.

I can share with you a few thoughts regarding happiness and marriage. Today the divorce rate is at an all-time high. The divorce rate has become so high that people are having prenuptial agreements created by an attorney. They are entering marriage with the mindset it may fail. The problem lies in that often the people getting married are unhappy people. When two unhappy people marry and depend on each other for their happiness, it is a recipe for disaster. I love my wife dearly but I don't expect her to provide my happiness. My wife brings me happiness, but she is not the source of my happiness. In the same manner, my wife loves me, but does not place the burden of providing her happiness on me. We are both individually happy and have the peace only God can provide. No other person can provide happiness for you. Happiness comes from a decision to be happy and to have a relationship with God. Marriage is tough and requires work. My love for my wife and my happiness with her is not based on the circumstances we face. My happiness in our marriage is based on a decision to be happy and a decision to love her.

Many situations in life can produce unhappiness. When people become unhappy and stay unhappy, they often eventually give up and being miserable becomes their normal lifestyle. What they are failing to realize is they have a choice in the matter. They can dust themselves off and take action. Sometimes in life you have to become sick and tired of being sick and tired. Getting out of the prison of unhappiness requires a decision and action.

There are times in life that people get into a rut and lose focus of their goals and dreams. In doing so, they end up settling for whatever comes their way. The hustle and bustle of life, along with stress and pressure has a way of wearing people down at times. Depression can cause you to feel too weak to even fight for the things you want out of life. Sometimes in life, you have to shake yourself and make a decision to take action. Good decisions and actions through faith can change your life.

There is a great story from the Bible in the 7th chapter

of 2nd Kings. I consider it one of the most interesting and motivating stories found in the Bible. In this story, the ancient city of Samaria in Israel was experiencing extreme famine. The famine was caused by a war that was taking place between Israel and the Syrians. The Syrians had surrounded the city of Samaria and were preventing any food from being brought out or taken into the city. Famine in Samaria was so intense women resorted to cannibalism and were eating their own children! The suffering in Samaria was indescribable.

When you read this story in the Bible, you will read about a day when four lepers were sitting outside the gates of the city of Samaria. In Bible times, people with leprosy were social outcasts and were rejected from contact with the rest of the community, and were driven out of the city. On one particular day in this story, the Bible says the four lepers were sitting outside the city gates contemplating their dilemma and their impending fate. They reasoned among themselves and one of them asked, "Why are we sitting here till we die?" Take a look at the passage from the Bible in 2nd Kings Chapter 7. This passage says, "Now there were four lepers sitting outside the city gates. 'Why sit here until we die?' they asked each other. 'We will starve if we stay here and we will starve if we go back into the city. So, we might as well go out and surrender to the Syrian army. If they let us live, so much

the better; but if they kill us, we would have died anyway.' "
(2nd Kings 7:3-8, Living Bible Translation)

The situation of the lepers in this story was grim. It required them to make tough decisions. These lepers knew they were sick and starving. They knew if they stayed where they were and did nothing, they would starve to death. They also knew if they tried to go back into the city, because they were lepers, nobody would have compassion on them. After all, they were lepers. The lepers made a bold decision. They decided to go to the camp of the enemy and surrender. They reasoned that the worst that would happen is that they would be killed. But, they knew they would die regardless if they did nothing. They knew they had to do *something*.

Sometimes in life, we get into desperate situations that require action and a decision. People often procrastinate in taking the actions that they know are necessary. Sometimes the delay in action is because of fear, or sometimes people are living in denial of the problem. Whatever the case may be, one thing is certain, if no action is taken, the crisis you face will not go away. A decision to improve your life must always be followed by action. You can choose to not be a prisoner of unhappiness. If you are already miserable, what do you have to lose? You can choose to allow God to take control of your life and give you the peace only He can give.

Maybe you are in a toxic relationship that is destroying you emotionally. Perhaps your health is not what it should be because of poor eating habits, smoking, or excessive drinking. Maybe you have tremendous financial problems, or have a job you hate. The possible scenarios and combinations of hardships in life are endless. Regardless of what problems you are facing in life, overcoming your problems demands decisions be made. Achieving happiness and becoming the person God created you to be begins with a decision.

When you read the story of the four lepers, you will find out that their decision to take action, and their refusal to just sit there and die brought change. God blessed them because they decided to take action and not settle in their misery. I don't want to spoil the end of the story for you. You should read the story yourself. It is one of the awesome stories from the Bible.

Problems and the stress that results from them can place you in a prison of despair. When you become imprisoned by stress and unhappiness, you need to praise God in spite of your situation. This is exactly what the Apostle Paul and Silas did when they were thrown into prison. In the 16th chapter of Acts, you can read about a time Paul and Silas were beaten and thrown into prison. They were in the inner prison.

During the time they lived, it was the equivalent of a maximum security prison cell of today. Despite their pain and seemingly hopeless situation, they praised God. They chose to look beyond their circumstances and thank God for his goodness and love. Their decision to not base their happiness on their situation brought about a miracle that changed the lives of others. Read the story. It will speak a great message to you.

Regardless of what you are facing in life, you have reason to be happy. We have a God who loves us and gave his son Jesus to die for us so that we may have eternal life. God loves you, has a plan for your life, and is able to do immeasurably more than you can ask or imagine. When you live life chasing happiness through circumstances, you will never find it. When you decide to be happy and completely trust God with your life, happiness will find you. Remember, happiness is a choice.

LESSON # 10

INVESTING IN OTHERS IS PRICELESS

Growing up, I was only concerned about me. I was an introverted kid with a damaged self-esteem wanting someone to notice me. Like everyone else, I wanted attention, love, respect, understanding from others, and encouragement. I spent years thinking my life was insignificant. My mistake was I was making life all about me. I wanted to receive, but didn't care about giving.

One of the greatest lessons I have learned is that true fulfillment in life comes from serving others and giving. I didn't understand giving as a kid. When I thought I wasn't receiving enough, or being served enough, I became discouraged. I was suffering from an "all about me" mentality. I never stopped to consider what I could do for others. I was only concerned with what others could do for me.

Today's society is saturated with people chasing after wealth, notoriety, and fame. The world today promotes a self-preservation attitude that says to look out for old # 1 first and worry about others later. The world today is filled with selfishness and greed.

The Apostle Paul warned his friend Timothy about how corrupt people would become in the final days before Jesus would return. Timothy was a younger man being taught and mentored by Paul. Paul referred to Timothy as his "son in the faith."

In a letter written to Timothy, Paul said, "You should know this, Timothy, that in the last days there will be very difficult times. For people will love only themselves and their money. They will be boastful and proud, scoffing at God, disobedient to their parents, and ungrateful. They will consider nothing sacred. They will be unloving and unforgiving; they will slander others and have no self-control. They will be cruel and hate what is good. They will betray their friends, be reckless, be puffed up with pride, and love pleasure rather than God. They will act religious, but they will reject the power that could make them godly. Stay away from people like that." (2nd Timothy 3:1-5, New Living Translation)

When reading that part of Paul's letter, I am amazed at how accurately it describes the world today. It is incredibly accurate because the words are from God, who knows all things. God knows everything that will happen throughout eternity. Paul wasn't predicting the future. Paul only wrote what God told him to write. In that same chapter of 2nd Timothy, Paul explained to Timothy that all scripture is inspired by God. Mortal men did not author the Bible; they merely recorded what God spoke to them.

Paul's letter painted a vivid picture of the self-centered, self-serving world we live in today. Mankind has evolved into people vastly different from who we were created to be. God intended for man to serve others rather than wait to be served. We were created to make investments into the lives of others.

God never intended for you to simply exist. Life is about more than eating, breathing, gaining possessions, and dying. I have heard it said when you die, the most important detail on your tombstone is the dash between the two dates. The first date tells when you were born. The last date tells when you died. The little dash between the two represents your time spent in life. It is the details of the dash that matter most.

God designed us to have a positive impact on the world.

God created within us the ability to give something back. The Bible says, "It is God himself who has made us what we are and given us new lives from Jesus Christ; and long ages ago he planned that we should spend these lives helping others." (Ephesians 2:10, The Living Bible Version) This scripture makes it clear we were created by God to be a blessing to others.

You have probably heard of the principle of sowing and reaping. This is not only a biblical teaching; it is a law of life. Even secular motivational speakers who don't profess to be Christians understand and teach this principle. The law of sowing and reaping says whatever you give you will get back. Think in terms of farming. If you plant corn you will eventually harvest corn. If you plant corn and expect to harvest wheat, you are in for a big disappointment. You can only harvest what you plant.

In life, you can only reap what you plant. Instead of the word plant, *sow* is the word the Bible uses. If you want more details on this principle from the Bible, read Galatians chapter 6. Sowing love will produce a harvest of love. If you sow bitterness or hatred you will also reap it. Problems arise when a person expects to reap anything other than what they sow.

Failing to understand the law of sowing and reaping causes people frustration, disappointment, and unhappiness. Many people sow rotten seed and wonder why their life is a wreck. If you want a quality life, you must sow quality seed. I compare it to people planting the cheapest grass seed they can buy and expecting a golf course type lawn. If you plant cheap grass seed you will end up with a lawn full of weeds. Life works the same way. Quality actions and choices make for a quality life.

You are continually sowing something. You are also continually reaping something. The choice as to what you sow and what you reap is entirely up to you. You have a say in the matter. The sowing that God intends for you to do involves investing into the lives of others. The most rewarding acts of sowing always focus on the needs of others. A farmer doesn't plant a crop solely for his own benefit and gain. His harvest can feed and help thousands of others beside himself.

Sowing into the lives of others works the same way. There is great personal satisfaction that comes from investing into the lives of others. My most fulfilling and rewarding experiences in life have come from striving to help others.

The mission trip to Africa my wife Janet and I shared together was one of my most rewarding life experiences. Forgetting your needs and pouring yourself into the needs of others is better than the high from any drug! The feeling that comes from showing love to someone in one of the poorest countries in the world is indescribable.

When I traveled to Burundi Africa, the words of Jesus from Matthew chapter 25 kept racing through my mind. In that chapter Jesus said, "When the Son of Man comes in his glory, and all the angels with him, then he will sit upon his glorious throne. All the nations will be gathered in his presence, and he will separate the people as a shepherd separates the sheep from the goats. He will place the sheep at his right hand and the goats at his left. Then the King will say to those on his right, 'Come, you who are blessed by my Father, inherit the Kingdom prepared for you from the creation of the world. For I was hungry, and you fed me; I was thirsty, and you gave me a drink. I was a stranger, and you invited me into your home. I was naked, and you gave me clothing. I was sick, and you cared for me. I was in prison, and you visited me.' Then these righteous ones will reply, 'Lord, when did we ever see you hungry and feed you? Or thirsty and give you something to drink? Or a stranger and show you hospitality? Or naked and give you clothing? When did we ever see you sick or in prison and visit you?' And the King will say, 'I tell you the truth, when you did it to one of the least of these my brothers and sisters, you were doing it to me!' " (Matthew 25:31-40, New Living Translation)

The words of Jesus from that passage in Matthew chapter 25 were of great comfort when I was in Burundi. I was reminded that the time I spent helping and ministering to the people I encountered was done as unto the God. The people I was able to help could not repay me, but my reward will await me in Heaven. Investing into the lives of others is sowing seed. In God's timing we will always reap a harvest of blessing from God. True giving is when we give freely expecting nothing in return. When you give in love and with a desire to help others, God will reward you in His time.

Everyone has opportunities and potential to sow and invest into the lives of others. My time spent in Burundi was a blessing and an experience I will always cherish. Missionary trips are wonderful and they will change your life. They will cause your priorities to change. Everyone should experience a mission trip at least once. But, please understand, a mission field is available to you every day; right where you live. You don't have to travel to another continent to invest in someone's life. You need only to look around you. There are hurting people everywhere. God can use you to sow good seed into someone's life. You can invest your time, your love, and encouragement to the people you see every day. Find someone to mentor and bless with the gifts that God has placed within you. When you do, you will create a great legacy.

As Jesus said in Matthew chapter 25, one day everyone will stand before God. It is then we will have to give account of the times we had opportunity to help someone and did nothing. I want to stand before God one day and say to him, "I used everything you gave me in the best way I knew how." In response, I want to hear him tell me, "Well done, good and faithful servant! You have been faithful with a few things; I will put you in charge of many things. Come and share your master's happiness!"

Throughout this book I have tried my best to share with you ten of my most important life lessons. My hope and prayer is that something you have read will help you. Never forget God has a plan and purpose for your life. Lessons we learn in life can propel us to become who God created us to be if we will allow God to speak to us through them. It is through God and the lessons of life we gain wisdom.

Benjamin Franklin once said, "Life's tragedy is that we get old too soon and wise too late." As God speaks to you through your mistakes in life, share the wisdom you have gained with others. In doing so, you can play a part in changing someone's life. Remember, what matters most is not what you leave *to* your loved ones. What matters most is what you live *in* them. Leaving a great legacy requires investing into the lives of others.

After reading this book, you may realize your relationship with God is not what it should be. Maybe you have never asked God to take control of your life and give you eternal life. That can change today! All you need to do is pray this prayer: Dear God, I realize I have sinned and I am not the person you created me to be. Please forgive me for my sins. I thank you for your love and for sending your son Jesus to die for me. Please come into my life, take what I have to offer you, and use me for your glory. Help me to leave a great legacy that honors you. In Jesus name I pray. Amen

ABOUT THE AUTHOR

Mark Lile is a Bible teacher, small group leader and mentor in his church, and a Christian blogger. He is a strong proponent of biblical stewardship through giving, eliminating debt, and living a debt-free life.

Mark and his wife Janet are entrepreneurs and have sponsored the construction of a medical clinic in the rural mountain village of Bukeye in Burundi, Africa. They also lead a debt elimination workshop at their local church.

Mark and Janet have four grown children and two grandchildren. They reside in St. Louis, Missouri.

For more information about Mark Lile visit his website at www.marklile.com.

Made in the USA
Middletown, DE
07 December 2016